Jungle Animals

Edited by Belinda Gallagher
Cover design by Oxprint Ltd.

ISBN 0 86112 719 6
Published by Brimax Books Ltd, Newmarket, England 1991.
Printed in Hong Kong.

LEARN ABOUT

Jungle Animals

Written by Jane and David Glover
Illustrated by Brian Watson

Brimax · Newmarket · England

Jungles grow in warm places along the Equator where there is plenty of rain. There are jungles in America, Africa, Asia and Australia. They are hot, wet and full of life. It rains nearly every day so jungles are sometimes called rain forests.

More kinds of plants and animals live in jungles than anywhere else on Earth. It is never quiet in the jungle. Monkeys chatter and howl, parrots screech, frogs croak and insects click and buzz.

The jungle trees are very tall and grow close together. There are always lots of leaves, fruit and flowers for the plant-eating birds, mammals, insects and reptiles. The plant-eaters are hunted by meat-eaters like eagles, snakes and tigers.

Down near the ground it is shady and still. Smaller trees and bushes grow between the jungle giants.

The okapi's stripes make it difficult to spot in the shadows. They help camouflage it from its main enemy — the leopard. The okapi uses its long tongue to pull leaves from the low branches.

The junglefowl feeds on seeds and berries. It is a close relative of farmyard chickens.

Tapirs feed at night. Their black and white coats make them difficult to spot in the moonlight. They roll in the mud to rub off biting insects.

Tigers are well-camouflaged, too. They hunt alone in the jungle. Their sharp hearing helps them find tapirs and deer.

The jungle floor is the home of gorillas and chimpanzees.

Gorillas may look fierce but they are intelligent and gentle. They live in families led by a big male.

During the day the family feeds on leaves and shoots. At night they make nests from branches and settle down to sleep.

The females have one baby at a time. The young gorillas spend lots of time playing with each other and with the adults.

Chimpanzees talk to each other with a complicated language of calls and signs. They hoot and shriek and drum on trees with their hands. If one chimp finds some food he calls through the forest to others.

In the branches above
the ground, hunters lie
in wait for their prey.

This jaguar is about to drop onto a tapir.
It is the third biggest cat after the tiger
and the lion. Sometimes it goes fishing –
scooping fish from the water with its
front paws.

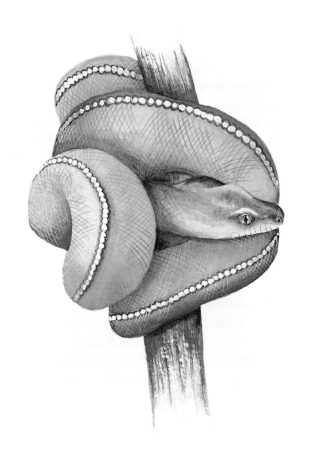

The emerald tree boa grabs its prey with its fangs – but it is not poisonous. It kills by coiling itself around its victim and squeezing until its prey suffo-cates. Then it swallows its prey whole.

Chameleons catch insects with their long sticky tongues. Their skins can change tone to match the background – so they are always well hidden from their prey and from snakes and eagles which might eat them.

Birds and butterflies fly between the trees.
But they are not the only flying animals in
the jungle.
The flying squirrel has folds of skin between
its front and back legs. When it jumps it
spreads them like wings. It can glide for
100 to 120 feet (30–40m). It uses its long
tail as a rudder to steer.

The flying dragon is a small lizard. It has flaps of skin which spread like fans to make wings. There are even flying snakes and frogs. Flying frogs have huge webbed back feet which they use like parachutes.
The flying snake spreads out its ribs to flatten its body. It then glides through the air after its prey or to escape from an eagle.

Most jungle animals live in the canopy – at the top of the trees where the leaves are thickest.

Sloths hang upside down from the branches. They move very slowly. They spend nearly 18 hours every day asleep or dozing.
The baby sloth clings to its mother with its claws, hidden in her shaggy fur. When it's six months old it wanders away to live alone.

The spider monkey is a very good acrobat. It swings and jumps from branch to branch using its tail like an extra arm.

Woolly monkeys live in large groups. As they feed they watch for enemies. Eagles take the young, and native tribes hunt them with blowpipes and bows and arrows.

Orangutans and gibbons are apes like gorillas and chimpanzees. But they live up in the trees – not down on the ground. They use their long arms to swing through the branches. Like gorillas and chimpanzees, they do not have tails.

Orangutans live on their own. They eat fruit, leaves, honey and eggs. A new-born baby

orangutan weighs just two pounds. It clings tightly to its mother's fur. She holds it on her hip with one arm. The baby stays with her until it is four or five years old.

Gibbons live together in small families with a male, a female and up to four young. They are very noisy – keeping in touch with loud calls as they feed.

Macaws live in groups. They are the biggest parrots in the world. They use their strong curved beaks to crack nuts. Macaws have no enemies except humans, who capture and sell them as pets.

Fruit bats feed at night. During the day they hang upside down in the tree tops. Bats are furry mammals like cats and dogs. They are the only mammals that can truly fly.

Hummingbirds and butterflies are attracted by the bright jungle flowers. They have long tongues to suck out the sweet nectar.

As they feed, the birds, bats and insects do a very important job. They spread the seeds and pollen that stick to their bodies, helping to start new trees and flowers.

The toucan lives in the tallest trees at the top of the jungle. It uses its long bill to eat fruits and berries. It picks a berry, tosses it in the air and catches it in its mouth.

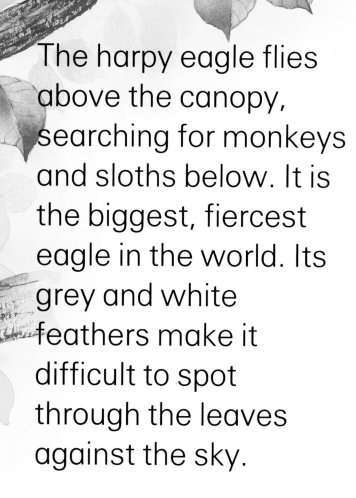

The harpy eagle flies above the canopy, searching for monkeys and sloths below. It is the biggest, fiercest eagle in the world. Its grey and white feathers make it difficult to spot through the leaves against the sky.

Many of the beautiful jungle animals in this book are in danger. Their jungle homes are being chopped down and destroyed by road builders and farmers. A lot of work will have to be done to protect the jungles or there will be nowhere left for these animals to live.

Jungle Animals Quiz

Now that you have read about jungle animals how many of these questions can you answer? Look back in the book for help if you need to.

True or false?

1. It hardly ever rains in the jungle.
2. Gorillas are gentle plant eaters.
3. Most jungle animals live on the ground.
4. Gibbons use their tails to swing through the trees.

Where do they live?

Where do these animals live in the jungle – on the floor, in the low branches, or in the canopy?

5. Sloth

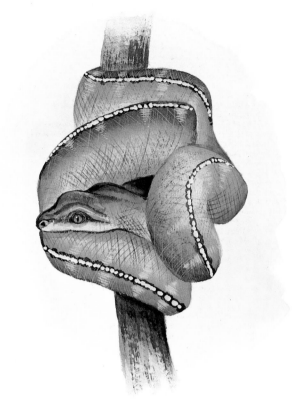

6. Emerald tree boa

7. Okapi

8. Toucan

Answers

1. False – it rains nearly every day.
2. True.
3. False – most jungle animals live in the canopy.
4. False – gibbons don't have tails.
5. Sloths live in the canopy.
6. Emerald tree boas live in the low branches.
7. Okapis live on the ground.
8. Toucans live in the canopy at the top of the jungle.